I GIVE MYSELF
PERMISSION
TO
PAUSE

HEALTHY LIFESTYLE

Habitat
Restoration
in Progress

BOUNDARY

SELF ESTEEM

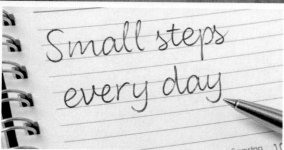

Small steps
every day

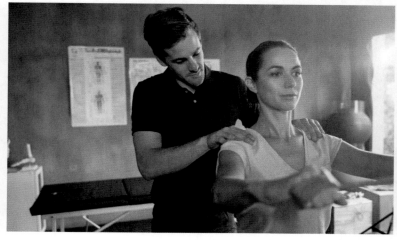

NOTE
TO
SELF !

LIVE
LOVE
LAUGH

SMILE :)

HAPPY

LAUGHTER
IS MY
MEDICINE

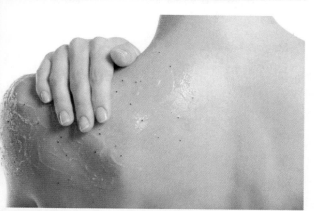

EAT HEALTHY

EXERCISE

SLEEP WELL

KEEP THINGS SIMPLE

THINK POSITIVELY

I **LOVE** MORNINGS!

NUTRITION

I
BALANCE
Work,
Rest
AND
Play

IMAGINATION

INSPIRATION

VISION

KNOWLEDGE

CREATIVITY

TECHNOLOGY

YOU MATTER

REDUCE STRESS

NO TOXIC FRIENDS

GO OUTSIDE

LOSE THE EGO

STAY ACTIVE

EAT HEALTHY

PLENTY OF SLEEP

ASK FOR HELP

NOW NEVER

BE YOU
DO YOU
FOR YOU

Safety by Choice, Not by Chance

SELF CONTROL

Just be your beautiful self

SELF-AWARENESS

I AM **GRATEFUL** TO BE ALIVE **TODAY**

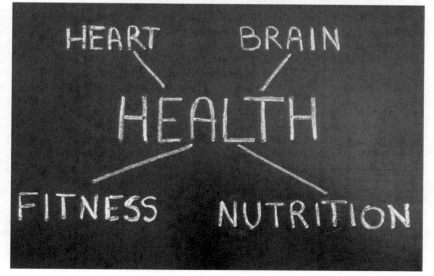

HEART   BRAIN
HEALTH
FITNESS   NUTRITION

Nourish Yourself
with the
Good Word

Zen

TIME TO HEAL

Harmony

nurture karma soul
pure holistic spiritual compassion
HEAL intuitive trust connect
WISDOM ask balance
accept believe receive
awaken unconditional love
ENERGY guidance
intention inner child
GRATITUDE forgive
divine GRACE release

HOPE
HEALTH
HEALING

Energy
Healing

Peace ♡
of Mind!

I
CHOOSE
TO LIVE WITH
GRACE

HEALTH
FITNESS
GOALS

Honesty   Trust   Respect

HEALTH

Strength

Exercise regularly

Reduce stress

Drink plenty of water

...t healthy

PEACE

WELLBEING

BALANCE

HARMONY

I CHOOSE
HAPPINESS

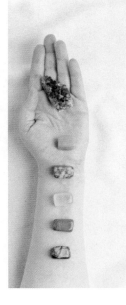

FITNESS

HEALTH

MY NEW
GOAL!
STAY FIT
WORKOUT

Sharper
Concentration

Better
Decision-
Making

Improved
Memory

Increased
Energy

Good Sleep

Improved
Physical
Health

Better
Immune
System

Ability to
Manage Stress

SLEEP
BETTER

don't stop
until you're proud

I AM
CONFIDENT
IN MY OWN
SKIN

take it easy

LOVE you

MEDITATE

LOVE

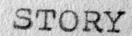

STORY

HOLISTIC

I **MOVE** MY BODY **DAILY**

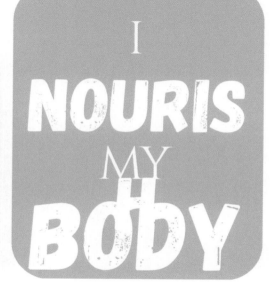

SUCCESS

JOY

find **JOY**

freedom

I BREATHE **DEEPLY** AND **FULLY**

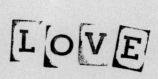

BE AUTHENTIC

I AM LIVING MY DREAM

FREEDOM

FAITH

DREAM IT DO IT

PEACE

DECIDE

HAPPY **THOUGHTS** CREATE A **HEALTHY** BODY

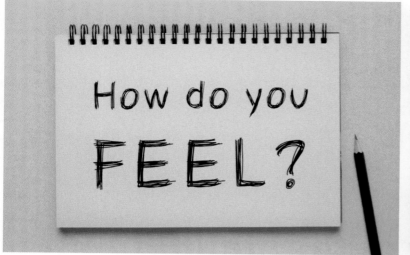

- ○ _____
- ○ _____
- ○ _____
- ○ _____
- ○ _____
- ○ _____
- ○ _____
- ○ _____

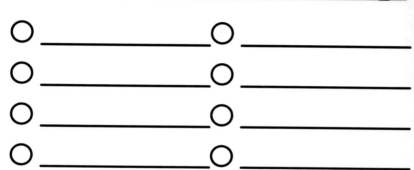

HOW DO YOU SEE YOURSELF IN TREE YEARS TIME?

Calm down

PRACTICE MIND FULNESS

gratitude

Breathe! You are alive!

I AM ENOUGH

SELF CARE

MAKE YOURSELF A PRIORITY

OVER THINKING

SELF CARE BUILDS CONFIDENCE

DIVINE SOUL RESPONSIBILITY consciousness
nonattachment willingness nonreaction
ENJOYMENT
ABUNDANCE ENTHUSIASM PURPOSE
AWAKENING PEACE NOW LET GO
I AM EGOLESS LIMITLESS transformation
AWARENESS

SLOW DOWN

I LOVE FEELING FIT AND STRONG

SELF CARE IS THE NEW HEALTH CARE

CREATE SELF CARE HABITS

HAPPY

I AM **FOCUSED** AND **MOTIVATED**

relation of
point of view.
Objective [
goal intended
to achieve and
based on obse

SHINE

BRIGHT

Mindfulness

I AM **SMART**
I AM **UNIQUE**
I AM **STRONG**
I AM **CREATIVE**
I AM **KIND**
I AM **BRAVE**

Take the first step. You can do it!

SELF-CARE

is

giving the world

THE BEST OF YOU

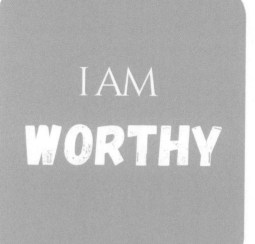

I AM **WORTHY**

YOUR
DAILY
ROUTINE
MATTERS

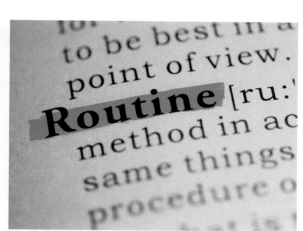

to be best in a
point of view.
Routine [ru:'
method in ac
same things
procedure o

FAMILY

OLD LIFE   NEW LIFE

Love
begins at
Home

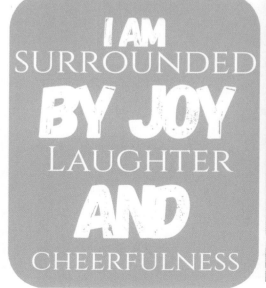

I AM
SURROUNDED
BY JOY
LAUGHTER
AND
CHEERFULNESS

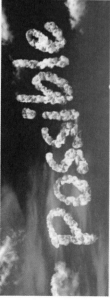

Positive

LIFE

Life VALUES

Family Happines	Generosity	Self-respect
Competitiveness	Recognition	Friendship
Spirituality	Wisdom	Advancement
Achievement	Health	Loyality
Affection	Responsibility	Order
Fame	Cooperation	Involvement
Culture	Harmony	Adventure
Wealth	Security	Pleasure
Serenity	Creativity	Freedom
Integrity	Power	Development

My top 3 VALUES

IDENTIFY YOUR VALUES

WRITE THEM DOWN

ACT IN ALIGNMENT WITH THEM

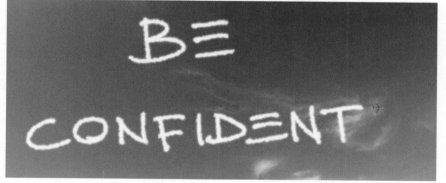

My *VISION* Statement

Thank you

for choosing our Vision Board Clip Art Book

As a special GIFT
I am offering you a
complimentary guide to
download.

This guide is designed to help
you confidently create your
vision board, set SMART
goals, and embrace unlimited
possibilities for your dreams.

Open the camera on your phone
(as if you're going to take a photo)
Hold the phone on the QR CODE below then
a link will appear on your screen
Tap on the link to get your FREE GUIDE

FREE GUIDE

Your Guide to
Creating the Life You
Dream Of

designed to help you clarify your values, align your beliefs, and set
actionable, meaningful goals that reflect your true self

Leen W.Hart

Much Love
Leen

Made in the USA
Las Vegas, NV
15 December 2024

14380567R00031